THE LOYALIST

Values and Gifts of the Enneagram 6

Asa Eccleston Kibilski

CONTENTS

UNVEILING THE LOYALIST: UNDERSTANDING THE CORE OF ENNEAGRAM TYPE 6

Welcome to the world of the Loyalist, the dedicated, responsible, and security-seeking individual at the heart of Enneagram Type 6. Known for their unwavering commitment to loved ones, causes, and beliefs, the Loyalist possesses a depth of character that is often underestimated and misunderstood. In this chapter, we embark on a journey to uncover the core motivations, fears, and desires that define this intriguing personality type.

The Loyalist's Quest for Security

At the very essence of the Loyalist lies a profound need for security. This yearning for stability manifests in various aspects of their lives, from their personal relationships to their careers, their finances, and even their worldview. Loyalists seek a sense of safety and predictability, a solid foundation upon which they can build their lives.

This desire for security stems from a core fear of being without support or guidance. Loyalists often worry about what might go wrong, anticipating potential threats and dangers. This hypervigilance can lead to anxiety, doubt, and a tendency to overthink decisions. However, it also fuels their remarkable ability to foresee problems and plan for contingencies.

The Gift of Loyalty

While the quest for security may be the driving force behind the Loyalist's actions, their most profound gift is their unwavering loyalty. They are fiercely devoted to those they love, their communities, and the causes they believe in. This loyalty is not merely a matter of duty or obligation; it is a deeply ingrained value that shapes their interactions with the world.

Loyalists are often the glue that holds relationships together. They are reliable, dependable, and always willing to lend a helping hand. Their commitment to others creates a sense of trust and belonging, fostering deep and meaningful connections.

The Loyal Mind: Thinking, Analyzing, Questioning

Loyalists possess a sharp intellect and a keen analytical mind. They are naturally curious, seeking to understand the world around them and their place within it. Their thought processes are often characterized by a thoroughness and attention to detail that can be both a strength and a challenge.

While this analytical approach allows Loyalists to make informed decisions and solve complex problems, it can also lead to overthinking and a tendency to get stuck in "analysis paralysis." Their minds are constantly churning, weighing options and considering potential outcomes. This can be exhausting, but it also allows them to anticipate potential problems and prepare for them.

The Loyal Heart: Feeling, Connecting, Belonging

Beneath the Loyalist's analytical exterior lies a warm and compassionate heart. They long for connection and belonging, seeking to build relationships based on trust and mutual support. Their loyalty extends beyond mere words; they are willing to put themselves on the line for those they care about.

This deep capacity for feeling makes Loyalists sensitive and empathetic. They are attuned to the emotions of others and often go out of their way to offer support and reassurance. However, their own emotional landscape can be complex, filled with both deep affection and underlying anxieties.

The Loyal Gut: Instinct, Action, Survival

Loyalists possess a strong instinct for self-preservation and a drive to protect those they love. This instinctual wisdom often manifests as a gut feeling or a sense of intuition. They are adept at reading situations and picking up on subtle cues that others might miss.

This instinctual drive can be a powerful asset, guiding Loyalists toward safe and secure environments. However, it can also lead to a fear of the unknown and a tendency to stick with what is familiar, even if it is not ultimately fulfilling.

Embracing the Complexity of the Loyalist

As we delve deeper into the world of the Loyalist, we will explore the many facets of this multifaceted personality type. We will examine the ways in which their core motivations, fears, and desires shape their relationships, careers, and personal journeys.

The Loyalist is not a simple or one-dimensional type. They are a complex blend of intellect, emotion, and instinct, driven by a deep yearning for security and a profound capacity for loyalty. By understanding the core of the Loyalist, we can unlock their hidden strengths, navigate their challenges, and celebrate their unique gifts.

THE THREE CENTERS OF INTELLIGENCE: HOW THINKING, FEELING, AND INSTINCT SHAPE THE SIX

The Enneagram provides a profound framework for understanding personality, and a key component of this framework is the concept of the three centers of intelligence: the Head Center (thinking), the Heart Center (feeling), and the Gut Center (instinct). Each center represents a distinct way of processing information and engaging with the world.

For the Loyalist, these centers play a significant role in shaping their experiences, behaviors, and perspectives. While all three centers are present in every individual, each Enneagram type has a dominant center that influences their primary mode of operation. Let's explore how these centers manifest in the Loyalist and how they contribute to their unique strengths and challenges.

The Head Center: The Loyalist's World of Analysis and Worry

Loyalists are primarily Head Center types, meaning their dominant mode of processing information is through thinking and analysis. Their minds are constantly active, seeking to understand the world around them and their place within it. They are naturally curious and inquisitive, often asking questions and seeking answers.

This intellectual orientation makes Loyalists excellent problem-solvers and strategic thinkers. They are adept at identifying potential issues, analyzing complex situations, and developing contingency plans. Their ability to anticipate and prepare for challenges is a valuable asset in both personal and professional settings.

However, the Loyalist's reliance on thinking can also lead to overthinking and a tendency to get stuck in "analysis paralysis." Their minds can become a labyrinth of what-ifs and worst-case scenarios. This can create anxiety, indecision, and a sense of overwhelm.

The Heart Center: The Loyalist's Quest for Connection and Security

While the Loyalist's primary focus is on thinking, their Heart Center plays a significant role in their lives as well. They long for connection and belonging, seeking to build relationships based on trust and mutual support. They are fiercely loyal to their loved ones and will go to great lengths to protect and support them.

Loyalists are often highly attuned to the emotions of others, empathizing with their joys and sorrows. They are natural caregivers and often find fulfillment in helping others. However, their own emotional landscape can be complex, filled with both deep affection and underlying anxieties.

Their fear of abandonment and betrayal can lead to insecurity and jealousy in relationships. They may seek constant reassurance from their loved ones, fearing that they will be left alone to face their anxieties. Learning to trust their own feelings and the love of others is a key growth area for Loyalists.

The Gut Center: The Loyalist's Drive for Safety and Action

The Gut Center represents the Loyalist's instinctual drive for self-preservation and a sense of safety. This center is often overlooked in Loyalists, as their thinking and feeling centers tend to be more prominent. However, their gut instincts play a vital role in their decision-making and actions.

Loyalists often have a strong "gut feeling" about people and situations. This intuition can be a valuable guide, helping them avoid danger and make choices that align with their values.

However, it can also lead to a fear of the unknown and a tendency to stick with what is familiar, even if it is not ultimately fulfilling.

Learning to trust their gut instincts while also balancing them with their thinking and feeling centers is an important step for Loyalists in their personal growth journey.

Integrating the Centers: A Path to Wholeness

While the Loyalist's dominant Head Center shapes their primary mode of operation, it is important to remember that all three centers are present within them. Each center plays a vital role in their overall well-being and functioning.

Integrating the three centers is a key goal for Loyalists. By learning to balance thinking, feeling, and instinct, they can access a greater sense of wholeness and fulfillment. This involves developing self-awareness, recognizing the strengths and weaknesses of each center, and learning to use them in a harmonious way.

For example, a Loyalist might learn to trust their gut instincts more fully, allowing them to make decisions without overthinking them. They might also work on expressing their emotions more openly, building deeper connections with loved ones. And they might find ways to quiet their busy minds, cultivating inner peace and tranquility.

By embracing all three centers of intelligence, Loyalists can tap into their full potential and live a life that is both rich and fulfilling.

THE HEAD CENTER: THE THINKING SIX'S WORLD OF ANALYSIS AND WORRY

Loyalists are often referred to as "the thinkers" of the Enneagram, and for good reason. Their dominant Head Center drives their relentless pursuit of knowledge, understanding, and security through analysis and planning. This chapter delves into the intricate workings of the Loyalist's mind, exploring their unique thought patterns, the benefits of their analytical nature, and the challenges they face when their thoughts run rampant.

The Thinking Six's Mental Landscape

The Loyalist's mental landscape is a bustling hub of activity. Their minds are constantly churning, processing information, evaluating options, and anticipating potential outcomes. They are driven by a deep-seated desire to understand the world around them and their place within it.

This intellectual curiosity fuels their love of learning and research. They are often drawn to fields that require critical thinking, problem-solving, and analysis. Their minds are like sponges, soaking up information and synthesizing it into a coherent worldview.

The Power of Analysis

The Loyalist's analytical nature is a valuable asset in many areas of life. Their ability to dissect complex issues, identify patterns, and develop solutions makes them valuable contributors in the workplace and trusted advisors in their personal lives.

Loyalists excel at planning and preparation. They are meticulous in their approach, leaving no detail to chance. This thoroughness can be a lifesaver in situations where careful planning is essential, such as organizing events, managing projects, or making financial decisions.

Their analytical skills also make them excellent problem-solvers. When faced with a challenge, Loyalists are quick to brainstorm potential solutions and weigh the pros and cons of each option. This methodical approach allows them to make informed decisions and navigate complex situations with confidence.

The Worry Trap

While the Loyalist's analytical mind is undoubtedly a strength, it can also be a source of significant stress and anxiety. Their tendency to overthink and overanalyze can lead to a state of perpetual worry. They may find themselves caught in a loop of "what ifs" and worst-case scenarios, unable to quiet their racing minds.

This constant state of worry can be exhausting and debilitating. It can interfere with sleep, relationships, and overall well-being. Loyalists may find themselves struggling to relax and enjoy the present moment, as their minds are always focused on potential threats and dangers.

Embracing the Thinking Six's Gifts

While the Loyalist's tendency to worry is a challenge that must be addressed, it is important to remember that their analytical mind is also a gift. Their intelligence, curiosity, and problem-solving skills are invaluable assets. By learning to manage their anxiety and channel their mental energy in positive directions, Loyalists can harness the full power of their thinking minds.

Here are some strategies for Loyalists to embrace their analytical gifts while mitigating the negative effects of worry:

- **Practice mindfulness:** By focusing on the present moment, Loyalists can quiet their racing minds and find inner peace.

- **Challenge negative thoughts:** When worries arise, Loyalists can practice questioning their assumptions and looking for evidence to support or refute their fears.
- **Set aside time for worry:** Designating a specific time each day to worry can help Loyalists contain their anxieties and prevent them from taking over their lives.
- **Seek support from loved ones:** Talking to trusted friends or family members can help Loyalists gain perspective and reduce their anxiety.
- **Consult a therapist or counselor:** Professional help can provide Loyalists with valuable tools and strategies for managing anxiety and developing healthy coping mechanisms.

By embracing their thinking minds and learning to manage their anxieties, Loyalists can tap into their full potential and live a life that is both fulfilling and meaningful.

THE HEART CENTER: THE FEELING SIX'S QUEST FOR CONNECTION AND SECURITY

Beneath the Loyalist's analytical mind and penchant for planning lies a deeply sensitive and compassionate heart. Their Heart Center, though not their dominant mode of operation, plays a significant role in their motivations, relationships, and overall well-being. This chapter explores the complexities of the Feeling Six's emotional landscape, their yearning for connection, the challenges they face in matters of the heart, and the path to cultivating emotional security and well-being.

The Feeling Six's Emotional Landscape

Loyalists are often characterized by their deep capacity for empathy and compassion. They are attuned to the emotions of others, sensing subtle shifts in mood and offering support and understanding. This sensitivity can make them excellent listeners, caregivers, and counselors.

However, their own emotional landscape can be a tumultuous terrain. Loyalists often experience a wide range of emotions, from intense joy and affection to profound fear and anxiety. Their fear of abandonment and betrayal can trigger feelings of insecurity and jealousy, while their desire for connection can lead to clinginess and dependence.

Navigating Relationships with the Heart

For Loyalists, relationships are a source of both comfort and anxiety. They long for deep, meaningful connections based on trust and mutual support. They are fiercely loyal to their loved ones and will go to great lengths to protect and nurture their relationships.

However, their fear of rejection and abandonment can create challenges in their interactions with others. They may overthink their partner's words and actions, searching for hidden meanings or signs of disapproval. They may also struggle to express their own needs and desires, fearing that they will burden or alienate their loved ones.

Loyalists often seek reassurance and affirmation from their partners. They want to know that they are loved, valued, and safe. This need for constant validation can be taxing on a relationship, but it is important to remember that it stems from a genuine desire for connection and security.

Cultivating Emotional Security

Emotional security is a cornerstone of well-being for the Feeling Six. They thrive in environments where they feel loved, accepted, and supported. However, their tendency to worry and their fear of abandonment can make it difficult to achieve this sense of security.

Here are some strategies that Loyalists can use to cultivate emotional security:

- **Develop self-compassion:** Learn to treat yourself with kindness and understanding, recognizing that everyone experiences fear and insecurity from time to time.
- **Practice mindfulness:** By focusing on the present moment, Loyalists can reduce anxiety and cultivate a sense of inner peace.
- **Communicate openly and honestly:** Expressing your needs and feelings in a clear and direct way can help build trust and intimacy in relationships.
- **Set healthy boundaries:** Learn to say "no" when necessary and protect your emotional energy.
- **Seek support from loved ones:** Talk to trusted friends or family members about your fears and insecurities.

- **Consider therapy or counseling:** A therapist can help you develop healthy coping mechanisms and build emotional resilience.

The Feeling Six's Path to Growth

The Feeling Six's journey to personal growth involves learning to trust their own emotions and the love of others. It requires developing self-compassion, cultivating emotional security, and finding healthy ways to express their feelings.

By embracing their sensitive hearts and developing emotional resilience, Loyalists can build strong and fulfilling relationships, navigate the challenges of life with grace and courage, and experience the deep joy and contentment that comes from living a life aligned with their values.

This chapter has explored the complexities of the Feeling Six's emotional landscape. We have seen how their yearning for connection, their fear of abandonment, and their deep capacity for empathy shape their relationships and overall well-being. By understanding these dynamics, Loyalists can embark on a path of personal growth and transformation, learning to embrace their sensitive hearts and cultivate a life filled with love, joy, and security.

THE GUT CENTER: THE LOYALIST'S DRIVE FOR SAFETY AND ACTION

While the Loyalist's Head and Heart Centers often take the spotlight, their Gut Center plays a crucial, though often underestimated, role in their lives. This chapter delves into the instinctive wisdom of the Loyalist, exploring how their gut instincts guide their decisions, actions, and pursuit of security. We'll uncover the strengths and challenges associated with this center, and how Loyalists can harness its power to navigate life's uncertainties with confidence and resilience.

The Instinctive Loyalist: A Deep-Rooted Survival Mechanism

At the core of the Loyalist's Gut Center lies a primal drive for self-preservation and a need to protect themselves and their loved ones. This instinctual wisdom is a survival mechanism that has evolved over time, helping humans navigate threats and ensure their well-being. For Loyalists, this manifests as a strong "gut feeling" or intuition about people, situations, and potential dangers.

This gut instinct can be remarkably accurate. Loyalists often have a knack for sensing when something isn't quite right, even if they can't articulate why. They may feel a sense of unease in a certain environment or a feeling of distrust towards a particular person. These gut feelings are not always based on logic or reason, but they can be incredibly valuable in guiding Loyalists towards safety and security.

The Power of Intuition

Loyalists who learn to trust their gut instincts often find that they make better decisions and avoid unnecessary risks. Their intuition can help them choose the right path, even when faced with uncertainty or conflicting information. By tuning into their bodies and paying attention to their gut feelings, Loyalists can tap into a source of wisdom that is often overlooked in our modern, analytical world.

This instinctual intelligence is not limited to sensing danger. It can also guide Loyalists towards opportunities for growth, connection, and fulfillment. By paying attention to their gut feelings, Loyalists can discover hidden passions, pursue meaningful careers, and build relationships that nourish their souls.

The Challenges of the Gut Center

While the Loyalist's gut instinct is a powerful asset, it can also present challenges. Their fear of the unknown can lead to a tendency to stick with what is familiar, even if it is not ultimately fulfilling. They may resist change, avoid taking risks, and settle for less than they deserve out of fear of the unknown.

Additionally, Loyalists may struggle to articulate their gut feelings to others. Their instincts may seem irrational or unfounded to those who rely primarily on logic and reason. This can lead to misunderstandings and conflict, as Loyalists may feel dismissed or invalidated when their gut feelings are not taken seriously.

Harnessing the Power of the Gut Center

To fully harness the power of their Gut Center, Loyalists must learn to trust their instincts while also balancing them with their thinking and feeling centers. This involves developing a deeper understanding of their own bodies and emotions, as well as learning to communicate their gut feelings in a clear and concise way.

Here are some strategies for Loyalists to tap into their instinctive wisdom:

- **Pay attention to your body:** Notice any physical sensations you experience when faced with a decision or situation. These sensations can provide valuable clues about what your gut is trying to tell you.
- **Practice mindfulness:** By focusing on the present moment, you can tune into your body and become more aware of your gut feelings.
- **Keep a journal:** Writing down your gut feelings can help you track their accuracy over time and develop greater trust in your intuition.
- **Talk to a trusted friend or advisor:** Sharing your gut feelings with someone you trust can help you gain clarity and perspective.
- **Take action:** Once you have a gut feeling, don't be afraid to act on it. Trusting your instincts can lead to new opportunities and experiences you might otherwise miss.

By embracing their gut instincts and integrating them with their other centers of intelligence, Loyalists can navigate life's uncertainties with confidence, resilience, and a deep sense of inner knowing. They can tap into their innate wisdom to make decisions that align with their values, pursue their passions, and create a life that is both safe and fulfilling.

WINGS OF THE LOYALIST: EXPLORING THE 5 WING AND THE 7 WING

While the core traits of the Enneagram Six, the Loyalist, remain consistent, their personality can be further nuanced by the influence of their wings. In the Enneagram system, wings are the neighboring types on either side of the core type. For the Loyalist, these are Type 5 (The Investigator) and Type 7 (The Enthusiast). Each wing brings its own unique flavor to the Loyalist's personality, creating subtle but significant variations in their behavior, motivations, and outlook on life. In this chapter, we delve into the characteristics of the 5 Wing and the 7 Wing, exploring how they shape the Loyalist's journey.

The Five Wing: The Duty-Bound Loyalist's Search for Structure and Support

Loyalists with a 5 wing, often referred to as "The Defender," exhibit a strong inclination towards knowledge, introspection, and a need for personal space. The 5 wing adds a layer of intellectual curiosity and a thirst for understanding to the Loyalist's already analytical nature. These individuals are often drawn to research, analysis, and solitary pursuits that allow them to delve deeper into their interests and gain a sense of mastery over their chosen fields.

The 5 wing also enhances the Loyalist's sense of responsibility and duty. They feel a strong obligation to their commitments, whether it be to their families, their work, or their communities. This sense of duty can drive them to great achievements, but it can also lead to burnout and a tendency to neglect their own needs in favor of fulfilling their obligations to others.

The Defender's strength lies in their ability to combine loyalty with intellect. They are reliable, trustworthy, and committed, while also possessing a sharp mind and a thirst for knowledge. This combination makes them valuable assets in any team or organization. However, they may struggle with emotional expression and a tendency to withdraw into their own world when feeling overwhelmed or stressed.

The Seven Wing: The Enthusiastic Loyalist's Balancing Act Between Fear and Fun

Loyalists with a 7 wing, known as "The Buddy," are often more outgoing, adventurous, and optimistic than their 5 wing counterparts. The 7 wing infuses the Loyalist with a love of fun, a desire for new experiences, and a zest for life. These individuals are often drawn to social activities, travel, and creative pursuits.

However, the 7 wing also brings its own set of challenges. The Loyalist's natural anxiety and fear of the unknown can be amplified by the 7 wing's desire for novelty and stimulation. This can lead to a constant internal conflict between their need for security and their desire for adventure.

The Buddy's strength lies in their ability to find joy and excitement in life, even in the face of uncertainty. They are often able to lighten the mood and bring a sense of optimism to any situation. However, they may struggle with commitment and a tendency to avoid difficult emotions.

Embracing the Wings: Integrating the Loyalist's Full Potential

Understanding the influence of the wings is essential for Loyalists to embrace their full potential. Each wing offers unique strengths and challenges, and by integrating both aspects, Loyalists can achieve a greater sense of balance and wholeness.

Here are some strategies for Loyalists to integrate their wings:

- **For the 5 wing:**

- o   Practice vulnerability and emotional expression.
- o   Make time for social connection and fun.
- o   Learn to balance your need for knowledge with your need for rest and relaxation.
- **For the 7 wing:**
  - o   Develop healthy coping mechanisms for anxiety and fear.
  - o   Practice mindfulness and grounding techniques to stay present.
  - o   Learn to set boundaries and prioritize your commitments.

By embracing both the 5 wing and the 7 wing, Loyalists can access a wider range of experiences, develop a deeper understanding of themselves, and live a life that is both rich and fulfilling.

THE FIVE WING: THE DUTY-BOUND LOYALIST'S SEARCH FOR STRUCTURE AND SUPPORT

When the Enneagram Six, the Loyalist, blends with the characteristics of the Five, the Investigator, a unique and compelling personality emerges – The Defender. This chapter explores the intricate interplay between the Loyalist's core traits and the Five's influence, revealing how this wing enhances certain strengths while presenting distinct challenges.

The Defender's Essence: Duty, Knowledge, and Introspection

The 5 wing infuses the Loyalist with a deep sense of duty, a thirst for knowledge, and a penchant for introspection. These individuals are often driven by a strong internal compass, guided by their moral principles and a desire to make a meaningful contribution to the world. They are reliable, responsible, and dedicated, always striving to fulfill their obligations to the best of their abilities.

Coupled with their inherent loyalty, the 5 wing's intellectual curiosity makes Defenders avid learners and researchers. They have a natural inclination towards acquiring knowledge and understanding the world around them. This thirst for information often leads them to pursue careers or hobbies that allow them to delve deep into their interests, becoming experts in their chosen fields.

Defenders are also highly introspective individuals. They enjoy spending time alone, reflecting on their thoughts and feelings. This introspective nature allows them to develop a deep self-awareness and a nuanced understanding of their own motivations and values.

Strengths of the Defender

The Defender's unique blend of loyalty, intellect, and introspection brings forth a multitude of strengths. Their strong sense of duty and commitment makes them reliable and trustworthy individuals. They are often the go-to person for advice, support, and guidance.

Their intellectual curiosity and thirst for knowledge make them excellent problem-solvers and critical thinkers. They are able to analyze complex situations, identify potential risks, and develop effective solutions. Their meticulous attention to detail and thoroughness in their work often lead to exceptional results.

Defenders are also deeply empathetic and compassionate individuals. While their introspective nature may make them appear reserved, they care deeply about the well-being of others. They are often willing to go above and beyond to support their loved ones and communities.

Challenges of the Defender

While the 5 wing enhances many of the Loyalist's positive traits, it also presents its own set of challenges. The Defender's strong sense of duty and responsibility can lead to a tendency to overwork and neglect their own needs. They may feel guilty for taking time for themselves or pursuing activities that are not directly related to their obligations.

Their introspective nature can also lead to isolation and social anxiety. They may struggle to express their emotions and connect with others on a deeper level. This can make it difficult for them to form close relationships and build a strong support network.

Additionally, the Defender's perfectionistic tendencies can be a source of stress and frustration. They may hold themselves to impossibly high standards, leading to feelings of inadequacy and self-doubt.

Integrating the Five Wing: Embracing Strength and Vulnerability

For Defenders to thrive, they must learn to integrate their 5 wing's strengths with the other aspects of their personality. This involves finding a balance between duty and self-care, knowledge and experience, introspection and connection.

Here are some strategies for Defenders to embrace their 5 wing while navigating its challenges:

- **Prioritize self-care:** Make time for activities that nourish your mind, body, and spirit. Remember that taking care of yourself is not selfish, but essential for your overall well-being.
- **Practice vulnerability:** Share your thoughts and feelings with trusted loved ones. Allow yourself to be seen and supported.
- **Connect with others:** Seek out social interactions and meaningful relationships. Find communities and groups that share your interests and values.
- **Embrace imperfection:** Recognize that everyone makes mistakes and that perfection is an unattainable goal. Learn to be kind to yourself and celebrate your achievements, no matter how small.
- **Seek support:** If you are struggling with anxiety, depression, or other mental health challenges, reach out to a therapist or counselor for professional support.

By embracing the strengths of their 5 wing and addressing its challenges, Defenders can unlock their full potential and live a life of purpose, passion, and fulfillment. They can become pillars of their communities, trusted advisors, and sources of inspiration for others.

THE SEVEN WING: THE ENTHUSIASTIC LOYALIST'S BALANCING ACT BETWEEN FEAR AND FUN

When the Enneagram Six, the Loyalist, merges with the traits of the Seven, the Enthusiast, a dynamic and captivating personality emerges—The Buddy. This chapter explores the fascinating interplay between the Loyalist's core anxieties and the Seven's zest for life, revealing a personality that thrives on both connection and adventure, while constantly navigating the delicate balance between fear and fun.

The Buddy's Essence: Enthusiasm, Optimism, and a Thirst for Adventure

The 7 wing infuses the Loyalist with a boundless enthusiasm for life, an optimistic outlook, and an insatiable thirst for adventure. These individuals possess a natural curiosity and a love of novelty, always seeking out new experiences and opportunities for growth. They are drawn to social gatherings, travel, and creative pursuits, often finding joy in the simple pleasures of life.

This infectious enthusiasm can be a source of inspiration for others, lifting spirits and fostering a sense of camaraderie. Buddies are often the life of the party, bringing laughter and levity to any situation. Their optimism and can-do attitude can be contagious, motivating others to pursue their dreams and embrace life's challenges with a positive spirit.

However, the 7 wing also brings its own set of complexities. The Loyalist's inherent anxieties and fears can be amplified by the 7 wing's aversion to pain and discomfort. This can lead to a tendency to avoid difficult emotions and situations, seeking distractions and pleasure to numb their anxieties.

Strengths of the Buddy

The Buddy's unique blend of loyalty, enthusiasm, and optimism creates a dynamic and engaging personality. Their infectious energy and positive outlook make them natural leaders and motivators. They are often able to rally others around a common cause, inspiring them with their vision and passion.

Their love of adventure and thirst for new experiences make them adaptable and resourceful individuals. They are able to navigate change with ease and are always open to trying new things. This flexibility allows them to thrive in a variety of environments and situations.

Buddies are also deeply loyal and committed friends and partners. They are always there to offer support and encouragement, and their optimistic nature can be a source of comfort and strength during difficult times.

Challenges of the Buddy

While the 7 wing brings many positive qualities to the Loyalist, it also presents its own set of challenges. The Buddy's fear of missing out (FOMO) can lead to a tendency to overcommit and spread themselves too thin. They may struggle to prioritize their commitments and may feel overwhelmed by the sheer number of options and possibilities available to them.

Their aversion to pain and discomfort can also make it difficult for them to face difficult emotions and situations. They may resort to avoidance tactics, such as seeking distractions or numbing their feelings with substances or activities. This can lead to a cycle of anxiety and avoidance, preventing them from addressing the root of their fears.

Additionally, the Buddy's enthusiasm and optimism can sometimes mask their underlying anxieties and insecurities.

They may project a carefree and confident image to the world, while privately struggling with self-doubt and a fear of failure.

Integrating the Seven Wing: Finding Balance and Groundedness

For Buddies to thrive, they must learn to integrate their 7 wing's strengths with their Loyalist core. This involves finding a balance between their desire for adventure and their need for security, their enthusiasm for new experiences and their fear of the unknown.

Here are some strategies for Buddies to embrace their 7 wing while navigating its challenges:

- **Practice mindfulness and grounding techniques:** By staying present and connected to their bodies, Buddies can reduce anxiety and cultivate a sense of inner peace.
- **Set boundaries:** Learn to say "no" to commitments that are not in alignment with your values and priorities.
- **Prioritize self-care:** Make time for rest, relaxation, and activities that nourish your soul.
- **Face your fears:** Rather than avoiding difficult emotions or situations, confront them with courage and compassion. Seek support from loved ones or a therapist if needed.
- **Embrace your full range of emotions:** Allow yourself to experience both joy and sorrow, excitement and fear. By acknowledging and accepting all of your emotions, you can cultivate greater emotional resilience.

By integrating the 7 wing's strengths with their Loyalist core, Buddies can unlock their full potential and live a life that is both exciting and fulfilling. They can become inspiring leaders, loyal friends, and passionate advocates for their causes.

SECURITY-SEEKING AT ITS CORE:
THE PRIMARY MOTIVATIONS
OF THE ENNEAGRAM SIX

The heart of the Loyalist's personality beats to a rhythm of security-seeking. This fundamental need for safety and stability underpins much of their behavior, decision-making, and worldview. In this chapter, we delve into the primary motivations that drive the Enneagram Six, exploring their deepest fears, anxieties, and the strategies they employ to create a sense of security in an uncertain world.

The Fear of the Unknown

At the root of the Loyalist's security-seeking lies a profound fear of the unknown. This fear manifests in a variety of ways, from a general sense of anxiety and unease to specific worries about finances, relationships, health, or the future. The unknown represents a lack of control, a potential threat to their well-being and the stability of their lives.

This fear can be both a source of strength and a source of limitation for Loyalists. On one hand, it fuels their meticulous planning, their attention to detail, and their ability to anticipate potential problems. On the other hand, it can also lead to overthinking, indecision, and a reluctance to take risks.

The Need for Guidance and Support

Loyalists often feel a strong need for guidance and support from others. They seek out authority figures, mentors, or trusted advisors who can provide them with direction and reassurance. This need for external validation can stem from a lack of trust in their own judgment or a fear of making the wrong decision.

While seeking guidance can be helpful in certain situations, it can also become a crutch for Loyalists. Relying too heavily on others can hinder their ability to develop their own inner compass and make decisions based on their own values and intuition.

The Desire for Certainty and Predictability

Loyalists crave certainty and predictability in their lives. They want to know what to expect, to have a clear plan, and to feel confident that their future is secure. This desire for stability can manifest in a variety of ways, from adhering to strict routines to seeking out stable and predictable careers.

While a certain degree of structure and predictability can be beneficial for everyone, Loyalists may take this to an extreme. Their rigid adherence to rules and routines can stifle their creativity and spontaneity. It can also make it difficult for them to adapt to unexpected changes or setbacks.

Strategies for Creating Security

Loyalists employ a variety of strategies to create a sense of security in their lives. Some of these strategies are healthy and adaptive, while others can become maladaptive and lead to further anxiety and stress.

Healthy strategies for creating security include:

- Building strong relationships based on trust and mutual support
- Developing financial stability and saving for the future
- Maintaining a healthy lifestyle through exercise, nutrition, and stress management
- Setting realistic goals and working towards them consistently
- Seeking out mentors and trusted advisors for guidance and support

Maladaptive strategies for creating security include:

- Overthinking and worrying excessively
- Avoiding risks and new experiences
- Seeking constant reassurance and validation from others
- Becoming overly dependent on authority figures or institutions
- Resorting to unhealthy coping mechanisms such as substance abuse or compulsive behaviors

The Path to Inner Security

Ultimately, the most sustainable form of security comes from within. While external factors such as relationships, finances, and career stability can contribute to a sense of well-being, true security arises from a deep sense of self-trust and inner peace.

For Loyalists, the path to inner security involves learning to trust their own judgment, developing their own internal compass, and cultivating a sense of self-worth that is not dependent on external validation. It also involves learning to embrace uncertainty and change, recognizing that these are inevitable parts of life.

By cultivating inner security, Loyalists can free themselves from the grip of fear and anxiety. They can learn to embrace life's challenges with courage and resilience, and they can find greater joy and fulfillment in their relationships, careers, and personal pursuits.

LOYALIST IN LOVE: BUILDING TRUST AND INTIMACY IN RELATIONSHIPS

Love and relationships are a central theme in the life of the Loyalist. Their deep-seated need for security, loyalty, and connection finds its most profound expression in their intimate partnerships. This chapter explores the unique ways in which Loyalists approach love, the challenges they face in building trust and intimacy, and the keys to cultivating fulfilling and lasting relationships.

The Loyalist's Love Language: Loyalty, Devotion, and Support

Loyalists are known for their unwavering devotion to their partners. They are reliable, dependable, and always willing to go the extra mile to show their love and support. Their love language often revolves around acts of service, such as cooking a meal, running errands, or offering a listening ear. They also value words of affirmation, physical touch, and quality time spent together.

Loyalists crave deep emotional connection and intimacy in their relationships. They want to feel safe, secure, and loved unconditionally. They are often drawn to partners who share their values and commitment to building a strong and lasting partnership.

Challenges in Love: Fear, Insecurity, and Overthinking

While Loyalists have a deep capacity for love and devotion, they also face unique challenges in their romantic relationships. Their fear of abandonment and betrayal can lead to insecurity and jealousy. They may overanalyze their partner's words and actions, searching for hidden meanings or signs of disapproval.

This tendency to overthink can create unnecessary tension and conflict in a relationship. Loyalists may become overly clingy or demanding, seeking constant reassurance and validation from their partners. This can be exhausting for their partners and can ultimately undermine the trust and intimacy that Loyalists crave.

Another challenge for Loyalists is their difficulty expressing their own needs and desires. They may fear that they will burden their partners or that their needs are not valid. This can lead to resentment and a feeling of not being truly seen or understood.

Building Trust and Intimacy: The Keys to Lasting Love

Despite these challenges, Loyalists are capable of building deep and meaningful relationships. The key lies in understanding their own needs and fears, communicating openly and honestly with their partners, and learning to trust themselves and others.

Here are some strategies for Loyalists to build trust and intimacy in their relationships:

- **Communicate openly and honestly:** Share your fears, insecurities, and desires with your partner. Don't be afraid to ask for what you need and express your appreciation for what you receive.
- **Practice active listening:** Pay attention to your partner's words and nonverbal cues. Show genuine interest in their thoughts and feelings.
- **Set healthy boundaries:** Learn to say "no" when necessary and protect your emotional energy. Respect your partner's boundaries as well.
- **Cultivate trust:** Trust is the foundation of any healthy relationship. Be reliable, dependable, and keep your commitments.
- **Show appreciation:** Express gratitude for your partner's love and support. Let them know how much you value their presence in your life.
- **Seek help when needed:** If you are struggling with

communication, trust, or other relationship issues, consider couples therapy or counseling.

The Loyalist's Journey to Love

The Loyalist's journey to love is a journey of self-discovery and vulnerability. It involves learning to trust their own hearts, overcoming their fears, and embracing the unknown. It requires open communication, mutual respect, and a willingness to work through challenges together.

By embracing their capacity for love and overcoming their anxieties, Loyalists can build strong and lasting relationships that provide them with the security, connection, and intimacy they crave. They can experience the deep joy and fulfillment that comes from loving and being loved unconditionally.

LOYALIST AT WORK: FINDING PURPOSE AND THRIVING IN A CAREER

The Loyalist's dedication, reliability, and strong work ethic make them valuable assets in the workplace. This chapter explores the unique ways in which Loyalists approach their careers, the challenges they face in finding fulfilling work, and the keys to thriving in a professional setting.

The Loyalist's Work Ethic: Dedication, Responsibility, and a Focus on Security

Loyalists are known for their strong work ethic and dedication to their responsibilities. They are reliable, punctual, and always willing to go the extra mile to ensure that their work is done well. They take pride in their contributions and are often motivated by a desire to make a meaningful difference.

For Loyalists, work is not just a means to an end; it is a source of security and stability. They value job security and often seek out careers that offer long-term stability and predictable income. They are also drawn to work environments that are structured, organized, and provide clear expectations and guidelines.

Challenges in the Workplace: Fear of Failure, Overthinking, and Difficulty Delegating

While Loyalists thrive in structured and predictable work environments, they can also face unique challenges in their careers. Their fear of failure and need for perfection can lead to overthinking and procrastination. They may struggle to delegate tasks, fearing that others will not do them as well as they would.

Loyalists may also have difficulty advocating for themselves in the workplace. They may be hesitant to ask for raises or promotions, fearing that they will be seen as greedy or demanding. This can lead to them being underpaid or undervalued in their roles.

Finding Purpose and Thriving in a Career

For Loyalists to truly thrive in their careers, they must find work that aligns with their values and passions. They need to feel that their work is meaningful and that they are making a positive contribution to the world.

Loyalists often excel in careers that require problem-solving, analysis, and attention to detail. They are well-suited for roles in fields such as accounting, engineering, law, healthcare, and education. They also thrive in roles that involve supporting and helping others, such as social work, counseling, and customer service.

Here are some strategies for Loyalists to find purpose and thrive in their careers:

- **Identify your values:** Take some time to reflect on what is most important to you in a career. What kind of work do you find meaningful? What are your strengths and skills? What kind of work environment do you thrive in?
- **Explore different career paths:** Don't be afraid to try out different jobs or industries to find one that feels like a good fit. Talk to people in different fields to learn more about their experiences.
- **Network and build relationships:** Connect with other professionals in your field. Attend industry events and conferences. Building a strong network can open up new opportunities and provide you with valuable support and guidance.
- **Advocate for yourself:** Don't be afraid to ask for what you need in the workplace. This includes asking for raises, promotions, or additional training.

- **Take care of yourself:** Maintain a healthy work-life balance. Make time for activities that you enjoy outside of work. Take breaks throughout the day to recharge and avoid burnout.
- **Seek support:** If you are struggling with work-related stress or anxiety, talk to a therapist or counselor. They can provide you with tools and strategies to manage stress and thrive in your career.

The Loyalist's Career Journey

The Loyalist's career journey is a journey of self-discovery and growth. It involves identifying their passions, honing their skills, and finding a work environment that supports their values and goals. It also involves learning to overcome their fears and insecurities, advocate for themselves, and build strong relationships with colleagues and mentors.

By embracing their strengths and addressing their challenges, Loyalists can build fulfilling and successful careers that allow them to make a meaningful contribution to the world. They can become respected leaders, trusted advisors, and valued members of their teams and organizations.

LOYALIST UNDER STRESS: RECOGNIZING AND MANAGING ANXIETY AND FEAR

While Loyalists are known for their stability and dependability, they are not immune to stress and anxiety. In fact, their deep-seated fears and anxieties are often the driving force behind their behaviors and decisions. This chapter explores the unique ways in which Loyalists experience stress, the common triggers that can set off their anxieties, and the strategies they can employ to manage their fears and cultivate resilience.

The Loyalist's Stress Response: A Spiral of Worry and Doubt

When faced with stress, Loyalists can easily fall into a spiral of worry and doubt. Their minds become fixated on potential threats and worst-case scenarios. They may start to question their own abilities, their relationships, and even their fundamental beliefs.

This heightened state of anxiety can manifest in a variety of ways, both physically and emotionally. Loyalists may experience physical symptoms such as headaches, stomachaches, fatigue, and insomnia. They may also struggle with emotional symptoms such as irritability, mood swings, and difficulty concentrating.

Common Stress Triggers for Loyalists

Several factors can trigger stress and anxiety in Loyalists. Some of the most common triggers include:

- **Uncertainty and ambiguity:** Loyalists crave predictability and control. When faced with uncertainty or ambiguity, their anxiety levels can skyrocket.
- **Conflict and confrontation:** Loyalists dislike conflict and

may go to great lengths to avoid it. However, when conflict is unavoidable, it can be a major source of stress.

- **Criticism and rejection:** Loyalists are sensitive to criticism and fear rejection. Negative feedback or disapproval can trigger deep-seated insecurities.
- **Change and transition:** Loyalists prefer stability and routine. Major life changes, such as moving, changing jobs, or experiencing a loss, can be extremely stressful.
- **Overwhelm and responsibility:** Loyalists often take on too much responsibility, both at work and in their personal lives. This can lead to burnout and overwhelm.

Healthy Coping Mechanisms for Loyalists

While stress and anxiety are inevitable parts of life, Loyalists can learn to manage their fears and cultivate resilience. Here are some healthy coping mechanisms that can help:

- **Self-care:** Prioritize rest, relaxation, and activities that bring you joy. Take care of your physical and emotional needs.
- **Mindfulness:** Practice mindfulness meditation or other grounding techniques to stay present and reduce anxiety.
- **Healthy communication:** Talk to trusted friends, family members, or a therapist about your fears and anxieties. Sharing your feelings can help you gain perspective and feel less alone.
- **Healthy boundaries:** Learn to say "no" to additional responsibilities when you are feeling overwhelmed. Protect your time and energy.
- **Exercise:** Regular physical activity can help reduce stress and improve mood.
- **Healthy diet:** Eating a balanced diet can provide your body with the nutrients it needs to cope with stress.
- **Sleep:** Getting enough sleep is essential for emotional and physical well-being.
- **Therapy or counseling:** If your anxiety is interfering with your daily life, consider seeking professional help.

A therapist can teach you coping skills and strategies to manage your anxiety.

Turning Stress into Growth

While stress can be challenging, it can also be an opportunity for growth. By facing their fears and learning to manage their anxieties, Loyalists can develop greater resilience, self-awareness, and emotional intelligence. They can also learn to trust themselves more fully and embrace the unknown with greater confidence.

The Loyalist's journey through stress is not a linear path. There will be ups and downs, setbacks and breakthroughs. But with the right tools and support, Loyalists can learn to navigate the challenges of life with grace and courage. They can emerge from difficult times stronger, wiser, and more resilient than ever before.

LOYALIST IN GROWTH: EMBRACING COURAGE, CONFIDENCE, AND SELF-ACCEPTANCE

Growth is a lifelong journey for every Enneagram type, and the Loyalist is no exception. While their core desire for security can sometimes hold them back, their capacity for loyalty, dedication, and hard work provides a strong foundation for personal development. This chapter delves into the Loyalist's path to growth, exploring the challenges they face, the opportunities for transformation, and the ultimate reward of embracing their full potential.

The Loyalist's Growth Edge: Stepping Out of Fear and into Courage

For Loyalists, growth often involves stepping out of their comfort zones and facing their fears head-on. Their anxieties can act as barriers, preventing them from taking risks, pursuing new opportunities, and fully expressing themselves. However, by confronting these fears, Loyalists can unlock a world of possibilities and discover a deeper sense of self-confidence and empowerment.

One of the key challenges for Loyalists is learning to trust themselves. Their reliance on external validation and their fear of making mistakes can make it difficult for them to make decisions without seeking reassurance from others. By cultivating self-trust, Loyalists can tap into their own inner wisdom and make choices that align with their values and goals.

Another area of growth for Loyalists is learning to embrace vulnerability. Their fear of rejection and criticism can lead them to build walls around their hearts, preventing them from forming deep and meaningful connections with others. By allowing themselves to be vulnerable, Loyalists can open themselves up to greater love, intimacy, and joy.

The Loyalist's Path to Confidence

Confidence is a quality that Loyalists often struggle with. Their anxieties and self-doubt can make it difficult for them to believe in their own abilities and worth. However, by facing their fears and taking on new challenges, Loyalists can gradually build confidence and self-esteem.

One way for Loyalists to boost their confidence is to focus on their strengths and accomplishments. They can create a list of their successes, both big and small, and refer to it when they are feeling discouraged. They can also seek out opportunities to use their skills and talents, whether it's volunteering for a cause they care about, taking on a new project at work, or pursuing a hobby they enjoy.

Another way to build confidence is to surround themselves with positive and supportive people. Loyalists can seek out mentors, coaches, or friends who believe in them and encourage them to reach their full potential.

Self-Acceptance: The Key to Inner Peace

Self-acceptance is a fundamental aspect of personal growth for Loyalists. They often hold themselves to impossibly high standards, striving for perfection in all areas of their lives. This can lead to feelings of inadequacy and self-criticism.

By learning to accept themselves as they are, with all their flaws and imperfections, Loyalists can cultivate a sense of inner peace and contentment. This involves recognizing that everyone makes mistakes and that it is okay to not be perfect. It also means embracing their unique gifts and talents, and using them to make a positive contribution to the world.

The Loyalist's Journey to Wholeness

The Loyalist's journey to growth is a journey of self-discovery, healing, and transformation. It involves facing their fears, embracing their vulnerabilities, and cultivating self-love and acceptance. It requires a willingness to step out of their comfort zones, take risks, and trust in their own inner wisdom.

By embarking on this journey, Loyalists can unlock their full potential and live a life that is both meaningful and fulfilling. They can become more confident, resilient, and compassionate individuals. They can build stronger relationships, achieve greater success in their careers, and make a lasting impact on the world.

The Loyalist's growth is not just about personal gain; it is also about contributing to the greater good. By embracing their strengths and overcoming their challenges, Loyalists can become beacons of loyalty, integrity, and compassion in a world that desperately needs these qualities.

INTEGRATING THE CENTERS: BALANCING HEAD, HEART, AND GUT FOR A WHOLE LIFE

The Loyalist's journey towards personal growth and fulfillment involves a delicate dance between their three centers of intelligence: the Head, the Heart, and the Gut. Each center offers unique gifts and challenges, and integrating them harmoniously is key to achieving a balanced and whole life. This chapter delves into the importance of this integration, exploring strategies for Loyalists to cultivate greater self-awareness, harness their strengths, and overcome their limitations in each center.

The Dance of the Centers: A Symphony of Intelligence

The Head Center, as we've explored, is the Loyalist's dominant mode of operation. It empowers them with analytical thinking, problem-solving skills, and a thirst for knowledge. However, an overreliance on this center can lead to overthinking, anxiety, and a disconnect from their emotions and instincts.

The Heart Center brings forth the Loyalist's empathy, compassion, and desire for connection. It allows them to form deep and meaningful relationships, but can also make them vulnerable to insecurity, jealousy, and a fear of abandonment.

The Gut Center provides Loyalists with their instinctual wisdom, a deep-rooted sense of knowing that guides their decisions and actions. However, this center can also manifest as fear of the unknown, resistance to change, and a tendency to play it safe.

Integrating the Head Center: From Overthinking to Mindful Awareness

For Loyalists, integrating the Head Center involves learning to quiet the noise of their thoughts and cultivate a greater sense of mindfulness. This means becoming aware of their thought patterns, identifying the triggers that lead to overthinking, and developing strategies to manage their anxiety.

Mindfulness practices such as meditation, yoga, and deep breathing exercises can be helpful for Loyalists to calm their minds and connect with the present moment. They can also benefit from engaging in activities that require focus and concentration, such as reading, writing, or creative pursuits.

Integrating the Heart Center: From Fear to Vulnerability

Integrating the Heart Center requires Loyalists to open their hearts to love and connection, even in the face of their fears. This involves learning to trust themselves and others, communicating their needs and feelings openly and honestly, and setting healthy boundaries.

Loyalists can benefit from exploring their emotional landscape through journaling, therapy, or creative expression. They can also cultivate greater empathy and compassion for themselves and others by practicing acts of kindness and generosity.

Integrating the Gut Center: From Fear to Intuition

Integrating the Gut Center involves learning to trust their instincts and intuition. Loyalists can start by paying attention to their bodily sensations and emotions, noticing how they feel in different situations and around different people. They can also practice making decisions based on their gut feelings, even if they don't have a logical explanation for them.

Engaging in activities that connect them with their bodies, such as dance, movement, or nature walks, can also help Loyalists strengthen their connection to their gut instincts. They can also seek out mentors or teachers who can help them develop their intuitive abilities.

The Reward of Integration: A Balanced and Whole Life

Integrating the three centers is not an easy task, but it is a worthwhile one. By balancing their Head, Heart, and Gut, Loyalists can achieve a greater sense of wholeness, inner peace, and fulfillment. They can tap into their full potential, make more informed decisions, build stronger relationships, and live a life that is both meaningful and joyful.

The journey towards integration is an ongoing process, requiring patience, self-compassion, and a willingness to embrace all aspects of oneself. But with dedication and commitment, Loyalists can achieve a harmonious balance between their thinking, feeling, and instinctive selves, leading to a life of greater authenticity, joy, and purpose.

EMBRACING THE GIFTS OF LOYALTY: CELEBRATING THE STRENGTHS OF THE ENNEAGRAM SIX

The journey through the complexities of the Enneagram Six, the Loyalist, culminates in this final chapter with a celebration of their unique gifts and strengths. While the Loyalist's path is often marked by anxieties and challenges, it is also paved with remarkable virtues that make them invaluable friends, partners, colleagues, and members of society. Let us delve into the treasures that lie within the Loyalist's heart and mind, and discover how their loyalty, commitment, and resilience can inspire and uplift those around them.

The Power of Loyalty: A Gift That Binds

Loyalty is the cornerstone of the Loyalist's character, a defining trait that permeates every aspect of their lives. Their unwavering devotion to their loved ones, their communities, and their beliefs is a testament to their deep capacity for love, connection, and commitment. This loyalty is not a fleeting emotion or a passing fancy; it is a steadfast and enduring force that provides a sense of stability and security in an unpredictable world.

Loyalists are the glue that holds relationships together. They are the friends who are always there to lend a listening ear, the partners who stand by their loved ones through thick and thin, the colleagues who can be counted on to go above and beyond. Their loyalty is a gift that not only enriches their own lives but also strengthens the bonds that connect them to others.

The Gift of Commitment: A Steadfast Path to Success

The Loyalist's unwavering commitment is another of their defining strengths. When they set their minds to something, they see it through to the end. They are not easily deterred by obstacles or setbacks, and their perseverance often leads them to achieve their goals.

This commitment is evident in their careers, their relationships, and their personal pursuits. Loyalists are not afraid of hard work, and they are willing to put in the time and effort required to succeed. Their dedication and reliability make them valuable assets in any team or organization.

The Strength of Resilience: Bouncing Back from Adversity

Life is full of challenges and setbacks, but Loyalists possess a remarkable resilience that allows them to bounce back from adversity. Their ability to cope with stress, adapt to change, and find meaning in difficult situations is a testament to their inner strength and determination.

Loyalists are not immune to fear and anxiety, but they have learned to face their fears head-on. They understand that vulnerability is not a weakness, but a strength that allows them to grow and evolve. Their resilience is a beacon of hope, inspiring others to overcome their own challenges and never give up on their dreams.

The Loyalist's Legacy: A Life of Meaning and Purpose

The Loyalist's gifts of loyalty, commitment, and resilience are not just individual strengths; they are qualities that contribute to the greater good. By living a life of integrity, compassion, and service to others, Loyalists leave a lasting legacy that inspires generations to come.

They are the mentors who guide and support others, the community leaders who advocate for change, the parents who instill strong values in their children. Their unwavering commitment to their beliefs and their dedication to making a positive impact on the world are a testament to the power of the human spirit.

Embracing the Gifts of Loyalty

The Enneagram Six's journey is not always easy, but it is a journey filled with meaning, purpose, and the potential for profound growth and transformation. By embracing their gifts of loyalty, commitment, and resilience, Loyalists can overcome their anxieties, build strong relationships, achieve their goals, and make a lasting contribution to the world.

This book has explored the complexities of the Loyalist's personality, delving into their fears, desires, and motivations. We have examined their strengths and challenges, their relationships, their careers, and their paths to personal growth.

As you close this book, remember that you are not alone. There are millions of other Loyalists in the world, each with their own unique gifts and challenges. By embracing your strengths, facing your fears, and cultivating self-love and acceptance, you can live a life that is both fulfilling and meaningful.